Forex Trading

PRACTICAL GUIDE to Dominate the Market: Strategies for Beginners, the Psychology to have Costant Results, Tips & Tricks

Michael Ross

The author of this book has taken careful measures to share vital information about the subject. May its readers acquire the right knowledge, wisdom, inspiration, and succeed.

Table of Contents

Introduction

Congratulations on downloading this book and thank you for doing so.

Money does not just drive the economy; it keeps everything in business. When you engage in forex trading, you deal with different currencies in the world. Many people want to learn how to trade currencies effectively but do not know how to start. This book was written not just to teach you how to trade currencies, but how you can do it effectively and in a way that allows you to rake in profits. The following chapters will teach you the "ins and outs" of forex trading:

Chapter 1 talks about the basics of forex trading to give you a good understanding of what forex is all about.

Chapter 2 discusses the advantages and disadvantages of forex trading.

Chapter 3 lays down the set of criteria to look for in a forex trading broker.

Chapter 4 reveals the powerful forex trading strategies that you can use to significantly increase your chances of success.

Chapter 5 talks about the best forex trading practices.

Forex Trading

There are plenty of books on this subject on the market, thanks again for choosing this one! Every effort was made to ensure it is full of as much useful information as possible. Please enjoy!

Chapter 1:
Forex Trading 101

What is *forex*?

Forex, also referred to as *foreign exchange* or *currency trading*, or simply *FX*, is the activity of trading currencies. This is important as it is what keeps businesses alive. It is also a driving force in the economy. Here is a simple example: Let us say that you visit India, you cannot pay the stores there in USD. What you need to do is to convert your USD into Indian rupees, the official currency in India. In the same way, the merchant has to pay using the right currency. In the given example, if the merchant gets his products in India, then he will most likely pay using the local currency; however, if he imports his products, then he will have to pay using the acceptable currency, which is probably the local currency of his supplier. As you can see, when it comes to business, there is a need to exchange one currency to another. This makes the FX market the largest and most liquid financial market in the world.

The world's currencies are traded on the forex market. It should be noted that the forex market is decentralized. Hence, do not expect to find a central marketplace. In fact, it does not even have a physical location. The trades happen online across a wide network of computers. If you want to trade currencies, then you simply have to access the Internet. Therefore, it is possible for you to engage in FX in the comfort of your home. As for the schedule, the market is open from Sunday (5PM EST) to Friday (4PM EST). It is noteworthy that the forex market is a continuously moving market, so you should keep a close eye on it.

The forex market can be classified into two groups: The interbank market and the over-the-counter (OTC) market. The interbank market is the market where banks trade, while the OTC market is where the regular traders engage in foreign currency trading. It is also worth noting that among the different currencies in the market, it is the USD that is mostly traded. 80% of all trades in the market include the USD.

The FX market is very active, which makes it a good choice for traders. However, it is also challenging to invest in currencies. It is not a secret that there are traders who lose their money in the FX market quickly. However, for those who know what they are doing, the traders who take the time and efforts to research and analyze the market, the FX market can be a goldmine of profits.

Why trade currencies?

So, why would you want to trade currencies? Well, engaging in FX is one of the best ways to make a profit. There are forex traders who are able to quit their day job and become full-time traders. You might be wondering just how much can you earn trading currencies? You can earn anything from a few dollars up to hundreds, thousands, and even millions in profit. The sky is the limit. However, trading currencies is also a kind of investment. Just like any other investment, there is also the risk that you might lose your money. In fact, if you do not understand what you are doing, then you will most likely lose your money. This is why it is important to first gain the right knowledge before you actually start trading currencies.

Forex pairs

When you trade currencies, it is a must that you understand what forex pairs are. They are the currencies that are traded. Major currency pairs in the market are the following:

EUR/USD

GBP/USD

USD/JPY

USD/CHF

USD/CAD

AUD/USD

There are also pairs that are not traded against the USD, so they comprise minor pairs. They are still liquid, but just not as highly liquid as the pairs that involve the USD. The minor pairs are:

GBP/JPY

EUR/GBP

EUR/CHF

Reading forex pairs correctly is important to a trader. Take note that in every pair, there are two currencies involved. Let us take the currency pair EUR/USD as an example. In a pair, there is the base currency and the quote currency. The base currency is the first currency in a pair. In the given example, it is the EUR. It is also called as *bid price*. The second currency is known as the *quote price*. In our example, it is the USD.

When trading currencies, there is a number after the pair. For example, it can be something like this: EUR/USD 1.25. Take note that the base currency, which in this case is the EUR, is always equals to 1. Therefore, you can view it as EUR 1/USD 1.25. This signifies that 1 EUR is equivalent to 1.25 USD.

Now, what if you want to use USD as your base currency? In forex convention, it will then look like this: USD/EUR 0.80. Be careful not to just switch the two currencies and their values. Instead, you have to divide the base currency by the quote currency. Although they may seem different, their mathematical relation remains the same. If you divide 1 by 0.80, you will get back to the value of 1.25.

Ask and bid

Let us now discuss the ask and bid price. Here is an example: EUR/USD = 1.3500/06. In practice, the difference between the ask price and the bid price is only a small amount. 1.3500/06 means 1.3500/1.3506. As you can see, there is a difference of 6 pips. For convenience, only the last two digits are written (06). Now, let me clarify a common misunderstanding. In forex trading, the bid price does not refer to the price that you offer to purchase a certain currency. Rather, this should be taken from the perspective of your broker. To earn a profit, a broker would ask higher than his bid price. As you can see, the difference between the bid and ask price is the profit that a broker makes from a transaction. It is referred to as a *spread.*

Types of orders

Knowing the type of order to give to your broker is important so that you can control how you enter and exit the market. If you want a successful career as a trader, then you should understand the different types of orders:

- Market order- This is the most common type of order that is used. It is an order to the broker to buy or sell a currency pair at the best price possible. This takes place in an instant and is made by the broker. If you want to enter the market quickly, then a market order is the way to go.

- Entry order- This is like a market order; the difference is that you get to enter the market only when the price of a currency pair reaches a certain point. You do not have to monitor the price of a currency pair all day long. You can set an entry price, and once the price of a currency pair reaches that entry point, then your broker will execute a buy order in your favor.

- Limit order- A limit order is used as an exit strategy. This order tells your broker to buy/sell a specific number of units of a currency pair at a specified value. If you are in a long position, then your limit order should be greater than the current price of a currency pair. If you are in a short position, then the limit order should be less than the market price. As a limit order, you set a limit line whereby a trade will be closed once it reaches that line. This can limit your losses and ensures your profits.

- Stop order- Just like a limit order, this is another exit strategy. The purpose of the stop order is to minimize your risk so as to limit your possible losses. With a stop order, a trade will close automatically once it reaches the limit that you have set. This is to avoid experiencing too much loss without having to monitor your computer all the time. If you reach your stop order, then it means that you have lost a trade, yet it is an effective way to prevent losing more.

Percentage in point

Percentage in point is commonly referred to as "pip." A pip refers to the measure of a spread. Remember that the spread refers to the difference between the bid and ask price. It is also how the broker makes money. The pip signifies a change in the value of as currency. You are probably familiar with how traders say that they want to profit by a particular number of pips, say 500 pips. What does this mean? Let us use an example: Let us assume that the price of a currency pair changes from 1.5000 to 1.5001. There is a change of 1 pip. A pip refers to the unit that the value of a currency pair changes. As a trader, you should by attention to the pip since it signifies how much you can profit or loss in a trade. As an example, let us assume that you buy the currency pair EUR/USD, you will profit if the price of EUR increases relative to the other currency in the pair, the USD. If you enter the trade and purchase EUR for $1.7600 and exit the trade at $1.7700, then you make a 100-pip profit. If the value of the pip decreases, then it will be a negative, which means a loss.

How many pips should you aim for? Well, there is no strict rule regarding this matter. It may depend on the strategy that you are using or the kind of trader that you are. Since currencies usually fluctuate slowly, the longer that you hold on to a particular currency pair, the higher is the probability that you can expect for more changes in price. For small or short trades, many are satisfied with a profit of just around 50 pips. This is a matter of personal preference. Just do what works for you. The important thing is to be in a positive profit when you finally add up everything.

Risk/Reward ratio

This is a calculation to know how much you need to risk in order to profit something. This way you will know if a certain trade is worth it or not. Here is an example: let us say that you trade with a stop loss of 13 pips and you have a take-in profit of 24 pips, then your risk-reward ratio would be 13:24. This means that you have to risk 13 pips to gain 24 pips.

The key is to look for a trade where you reward will be much higher than your risk. The most ideal is to find a trade that has a high reward and a low risk, although this is not always possible. There are no hard and fast rules as to what constitutes an ideal ratio. It will depend on the kind of trader you are and the strategy that you use, as well as your ability to manage risks. As a trader, your job is to look for a trade where the reward outweighs your risks.

Leverage

This is one of the reasons why people love to engage in forex. FX trading allows them to leverage their position. So, what does this mean? Leveraging is where you borrow money from your broker. Hence, you can invest and trade a larger amount. Of course, this translates to having a higher potential profit. The good news is that forex is known for having a high leverage. This means that even with a small margin, you can trade a high amount. The degree of leverage can vary, such as 50:1, 100:1, even 200:1. This will depend on your broker, as well as the size of your position. So, what do these numbers mean? A 50:1 leverage signifies that the minimum margin requirement is only 2% (1/50) of the total value of trade in his trading account available as cash. Accordingly, a 1:100 leverage would only require 1%, and so on. The usual leverages used as 1:50 and 1:100. A leverage of 1:200 is used normally for positions that are around $50,000 or less. In application, this means that if you intend to trade $100,000 with a margin of 1%, then you only need to risk $1,000. Although a leverage of 100:1 is risky, keep in mind that currencies do not fluctuate very high. In fact, normally, they fluctuate by less than 1% in a day.

Obviously, the main advantage of leveraging is that it allows you to have a decent trade size even if you only have a small start-up capital. And, even if you have a big fund for trading, it can further expand it, allowing you to profit even more. However, just be careful, because leveraging also has a catch. After all, no broker would lend you money just for nothing. So, what is the catch? Well, since you will be borrowing funds from your broker, you have to pay interest. You should take note of this interest since you need to pay your broker to continue making use of the leverage. Needless to say, you also have a choice not to leverage your position so that you would not worry about paying interest to your broker.

Day Trading Vs. Long-term Trading

Another important part of making a successful trade is learning how long to hold on to your position. Remember that a trade is composed of two parts: You have to enter the market (buy), and then exit the market (sell). How long you intend to hold on to your position depends on your preference. There are traders who open and close out all their positions in one trading day. This activity is known as day trading. A good thing about day trading is that you get to start with a clean slate every day. You are also not exposed to the risks of continuous decrease in the prices of currencies. By closing your positions within one trading day, you prevent yourself from continuously holding on to a losing currency pair. If you want to make money quickly, then you can try day trading. However, day traders need to be very active. Since you open and close out all positions in one trading day, you need to keep a close eye on the market. You also need to be more consistent in doing research and analysis. Day trading can also be stressful since you have to deal with a fast-paced environment. If you do not understand what you are doing, then this is a quick way to lose all of your funds. Short-term trades are also easily affected by the mere volatility of the market. Although price volatility is a normal part of the market, it can have serious effects when you do day trading.

Now, let us take a look at another kind of trading known as long-term trading. Long-term trading revolves around the buy and holds strategy. In this case, you buy a currency pair, you keep it for some time as its price increases, and then you sell it for profit. When you do long-term trading, you do not have to worry about the day-to-day volatility in the market. You also do not have to pressure yourself to make a trade every day.

You are free do all the research you want and feel free to enter and exit the market as you please. Since you can hold on to a currency pair for a longer period, you can also earn a nice profit. Most long-term traders also do not make many trades. In fact, many long-term traders only make a few trades. As such, they do not have to do as much research as day traders. However, take note that this does not mean that doing research is no longer important. You still need to follow how the market moves. Long-term trading also has more chances to recover from a bad trade. Remember that the prices of currencies fluctuate continuously. Hence, just because it appears that a particular trade is at a loss does not mean that it will continue to be a losing trade. There is still a chance that it may recover and make a profit for you.

So, which kind of trading approach is better? There is no hard and fast rule on this matter. Rather, it will depend on the strategy that you use. There are those who make a profit with day trading, while there are also those who prefer to use long-term trading. Some others apply both as they see fit. This is up to you to decide. So, try what works best for you and stick to it.

Trading psychology

As a trader, it is also important that you understand trading psychology. So, what happens in the mind of a trader? When you engage in forex trading, having the right mindset is important.

- Be objective- When you work as a forex trader, there are times when you might be controlled by your emotions. Remember to always be objective. The market does not care how you feel. This is an important part of being a trader. Never allow your emotions to make decisions for you. To ensure that you are being objective, you should make sure that every decision that you make is backed up by a solid research and analysis. You must have good reasons to support your trading decisions.

- Greed- Greed has caused so many traders and gamblers to lose their money. Although it is good to have a desire to make a profit, you should not let this desire get out of control. A good way to prevent falling into this trap is by setting a clear objective and sticking to it. For example, if your objective is to earn 5% in a trade, then close your position once you reach your objective. Sometimes it is by holding on for too long to a trade that can cause you to lose money. Never allow greed to take away your profits. Exercise self-discipline.

- Focus on quality over quantity- It is very tempting to make multiple trades. Just remember to always pay attention to the quality of your trades. Make sure that every trade you make is backed up with sufficient amount of research. A common mistake is to take the profitability of some trades for granted thinking that you have many funds that you can use. Remember that it is better not to enter into any trade than to make a trade that is poorly made. It is not uncommon to find professional traders who only open a few trading positions. Remember that it is not the number of trades that you have that matters but whether or not your trades will end up in a profit.

- Panic- Panic is very common, especially for inexperienced traders. It usually takes place when the market falls unexpectedly. The tendency is that out of panic, traders will pull out of their positions which can further aggravate the situation in the market. Experienced traders know better and know that such unexpected drop in value happens from time to time, and so it no longer catches them off guard; they know that the market is volatile and so they are ready for any kind of change. Experienced traders know that no good can come from being controlled by a situation and panicking. Instead of being controlled by the situation, you should relax and take a closer look at the market. This way you will see things more clearly, and you will not respond rashly. Just because other traders are panicking does not mean that you should also do the same. A mark of a well-trained and experienced trader is the ability to remain calm despite difficult situations. When the market is in panic, it will be easy to read how the people will respond. If you remain calm and objective, you can use this situation to your advantage.

- Fear- Fear can be said to be the opposite of greed. In this case, you fail to take full advantage of a profitable position for fear that you might lose your money. The way to win against fear (and greed) is by acquiring the right knowledge. Fear often arises out of ignorance. This is another reason why doing research is very important for forex traders. It is by doing research that you can acquire the right information and help you to understand the market situation more clearly. In turn, it will allow you to make wise trading decisions. You should strike a good balance between fear and greed. To do this, you need to focus on gaining knowledge.

- Overconfidence- Being overconfident is a common yet serious blunder that you should avoid. This usually happens after you make a series of successful trades. The tendency is to get too confident and start to do less research. Remember never to be too confident. Being confident is good but being overly confident can make you lose your money. Also, being overly confident can lead to greed. As you already know, you should never submit to greed. As you can see, overconfidence in itself is not really bad. Rather, it is what you tend to do when you are overconfident that is not good. If you ever notice that you are being overconfident, then you should stop making trades and just relax. Be calm and take a closer look at the market.

- Self-control- Successful traders have a great deal of self-control. They do not allow themselves to be attached to their trades. They can even laugh at some losing trades. This is because they have already realized that in a course of a trading career, encountering losing trades is normal. They also exercise self-control at all times and refuse to submit to fear and/or greed. This is how they maintain the right mindset for trading. Of course, having self-control may not be easy, especially when you are just starting out, but it is nonetheless doable as long as you persist. It is easy to get carried away when you trade currencies, especially when your emotions start to be involved. This is not good because it prevents you from thinking clearly and objectively. Hence, it is extremely important that you learn to control yourself.

- Bias- This is another negative mindset to watch out for. Unfortunately, many traders are biased when making a trade. They simply prefer certain pairs more than others. The problem is that they have no good reason to feel this way. Just because you pick a particular pair does not mean that it has a higher chance at making a profit. You should see things fairly as they are. This is how you can come up with a good and fair decision. It is not just about what you like that matters. You need to objectively consider the situation of the market. Do not be attached to your trades and your decisions. Instead, view them as you would other people's trades. When you know that they are your own positions, there is a tendency to be biased and see them to be better than they actually are. Do not allow yourself to be attached to anything and see things as they are.

Chapter 2:
Advantages and Disadvantages

<u>Advantages</u>

- High profit- Trading currencies has a high-profit potential. In fact, there are people who have attained financial freedom by trading currencies alone. Also, since you can leverage your position, even a small investment of $100 can go a long way. But, of course, you need to know and understand what you are doing. With currency trading, you can earn even as high as 400% in a short period of time.

Compare this with trading stocks where a profit of 30% in a year is considered high. When you engage in the FX market, there is no limit to how much you can earn. Hence, if you have money to spare, it is strongly suggested that you give forex trading a try.

- Leverage- Forex trading allows you to leverage your position. As we have already discussed, by leveraging your position, you can invest a small amount of money but be able to trade with much bigger funds. Obviously, this allows you to rake in more profits. By taking advantage of leveraging, you can earn a high amount of profits by risking less money of your own. Now, if you invest a big amount, just imagine how much more you can earn. Of course, you are also free to decide not to leverage your position. This will be discussed in more detail later in the book.

- High liquidity- The forex market is known for having a high liquidity. This means that you can easily buy and sell currencies, as you can always find someone who would take the other side of a trade that you make. It is an active market, and you can buy and sell currencies at any time.

- Low cost- Unlike other investments where you will have to worry about surcharges and other fees, the costs in forex trading are normally already included in the spread. Even the retail transaction cost is also normally below 0.1%. even if you work with a big dealer, the cost is almost always less than 1%. But, of course, this will depend on the leverage that you pick. Since you do not have to worry about having to deal with different costs, you can put more focus on what really matters, and that is making profitable trading decisions.

- Round-the-clock market- When the market opens, you can be sure that it will remain open until the close of the trading week. Feel free to make trades in the morning, afternoon, evening, or at any time that you want.

- Fair market - There is no central authority that controls the FX market. Although there are things that can affect the market, they cannot control the market for an extended period of time. The market is also filled with many participants, and no one is more favored than another.

- Easy to enter- It is not hard to enter the FX market. All you need to do is to go online, make an account with a reliable broker, put even a little investment, and you can start trading. You can do all these things in the comfort of your home with just a few clicks of a mouse.

- More choices- With more than 25 currency pairs that you can choose from, you will definitely not run out of choices to trade. You will not have to worry about sitting idly as there is always an open opportunity for you to make a profit. All you need is to make the right trading decisions. Having more choices allows you to have more opportunities to make money.

- Fun- Last but not least, trading currencies can be fun. In fact, it is not uncommon for traders not to notice how time passes by as they make trades or prepare to make trades. Indeed, the activities of a forex trader can be very entertaining, interesting, and challenging, all at the same time. This is why you can find many traders who have become addicted to what they are doing.

Disadvantages

- Risky- It is true that people trade currencies to make a profit; however, it is also true that many currency traders lose their money. It is can be really risky to engage in the forex market, especially if you do not understand what you are doing. If you trade currencies without the right foundation and preparation, then you will most likely lose your money. Well-experienced traders use much caution even in opening a position, and so you should be all the more careful since you are a beginner. Also, there is no amount of research and preparation that can guarantee the return of positive profits; there are always risks involved.

- High volatility- There are many factors that affect the prices of currencies. Indeed, the forex market can be highly volatile. You can also expect unforeseeable events to take place. Unfortunately, traders cannot do anything to prevent such things from happening. When Iceland was bankrupt, traders who were holding Icelandic krona could not do anything about it. They could only watch as the price of the currency that they were holding dropped. To limit your losses, you should make sure to always do your research before you enter any trading position and always apply an effective strategy.

- Does not offer the highest return- Although you can make a high amount of profit when you trade currencies, it is true that forex trading still does not offer the highest rate of return. For example, trading binary options can give you a profit return of 90% in just a few minutes. When you trade currencies, it will take more than a day for you to earn a 90% profit. However, unlike binary options trading, forex is less risky.

- You are on your own- When you invest in stocks, you can ask for assistance from trade advisors as well as trade managers to help you come up with a sound investing/trading decision. When you trade foreign currencies, you have no one to turn to. You will have to make all the decisions by yourself. This is why it is not uncommon for new traders to lose their money. If you are just starting out, it is strongly advised that you take advantage of the demo account provided by your broker. It is a good way to be familiar with the real trading environment without risking real money.

- Difficult to predict- Although there are strategies that you can use, and although you can spend all the hours you want to predict the forex market, the fact remains that you can never have a 100% guarantee that your investment will give you a positive profit return. There are many things that can affect the price of a currency, and many of these things are outside of your control.

- Less regulated- There is no central authority that regulates the forex market. If you want to trade currencies, you will have to deal with a forex trading broker. It is important that you work only with a reliable broker. Unfortunately, there are many scammers online who want to rip you off. Since you will be relying on a broker, you will not be in total control of your trades. The takeaway message is to always be careful with choosing your forex broker.

Chapter 3:
Things to Look for in a Forex Trading

Set of Criteria to Look for in a Forex Trading Broker

Before you can start trading currencies, you need to sign up for an account with a forex trading broker. It is extremely important that you work with a reliable broker. Just a word of caution: There are many scammers online, so you need to be diligent and exercise extra caution in choosing a broker. Now, when you do a search online, you will find many forex brokers. SO, how do you identify the one that will best suit your needs? To help you choose a trustworthy broker, here are the criteria to look for:

- Ratings and reviews- Before making any real money deposit, be sure to check the latest ratings and reviews of a broker. This is easy to do. Simply use your favorite search engine, type the name of the broker in the search box and add the word "reviews." The search engine results pages (SERP) will then show you related pages. Be sure to read the reviews and ratings given to the broker from different websites. Also, do not forget to compare its reviews with the reviews given to other forex brokers. You should also pay attention to the dates when the reviews were made. If the latest reviews were made over a year ago, then you should be extra careful. It is also worth noting that the best forex brokers yesterday may no longer be the best today. After all, the management team of a broker may change at any time.

- Customer support- It is important that you work with a broker that has an active and reliable customer support. In the course of trading, you will definitely encounter issues, especially technical issues, from time to time. When this happens, there is no one else whom you can rely on but the broker's customer support team. You can direct your questions regarding the trading platform, technical issues, or otherwise, to customer support.

Take note of the ways that you can get in touch with customer support. Normally, there will be a page on the broker's website where you can send a message to the customer support or at least an email address that you can send a message to. Some brokers will even provide a phone number that you can call at any time, while others will allow you to have an on-page chat with the support team.

- Cost of transaction- Normally, a broker imposes its charge on the spread and no longer charges additional costs. However, some brokers make money on a commission basis by getting a percentage from the spread. Before you make any deposit, find out if the broker imposes a charge on a per-spread basis or on commission.

- Trading platform- Take note that it is your broker that will provide you with a platform that you can use to trade currencies. Your forex broker should at least provide you with graphs and related tools that you can use to make technical analysis. Although not a requirement, it is still a big plus if the platform is professionally designed as this can help set you up for better success in trading. The platform should make the experience of trading easy and convenient for you. It should enable you to trade quickly and easily with just a few clicks of the mouse. It is suggested that you take advantage of the demo account provided by your forex broker to find out if the platform is suitable for your needs and preferences.

- Banking options- Before making any real money deposit, you should take note of the banking options provided by your broker. It is not uncommon to find a broker that offers more options for making a deposit but only limited options for making a withdrawal. It is also common for brokers to request certain identity documents before they process a withdrawal. Make sure that you know these documents and that you have them in your possession. Otherwise, you run the risk of having your funds locked in your account without any way of withdrawing them. If you have concerns regarding this matter, feel free to contact the support team.

- Currency pairs available- Not all brokers offer the same number of currency pairs. Of course, the more currency pairs offered by your broker, the more choices that you will have. Your broker must at least have the major currency pairs, such as the EUR/USD, USD/JPY, USD/CHF, and GBP/USD. Of course, traders may also have a certain interest in a particular currency pair which may not even be considered as a major currency pair. In such case, the important thing is for your broker to offer the currency pair that you are interested in. Remember that a good broker will make the experience of trading currencies easy and more convenient and not the other way around.

- Bonuses- It is not uncommon for brokers to offer bonuses. Normally, brokers use bonuses to attract traders to sign up for an account with them. Accepting a bonus is a good way to earn free money that you can use for trading. However, it should be noted that before you accept any bonus or promotion, you need to read and understand the terms of accepting the said bonus. There is usually a catch involved. For example, A broker may tempt you to make a deposit by offering a bonus of 50%. This means that if you deposit $100, then you will have a total of $150 in your trading account. However, the drawback is that a forex broker will impose a wagering requirement once you accept a bonus. After all, no forex broker will just give you free money for nothing. Therefore, before you accept a bonus, make sure that you read the terms and conditions that go with it.

Chapter 4:
Powerful Forex Trading Strategies

If you want to have continuous success with forex trading, you cannot just rely on luck. Instead, you need to learn and use effective trading strategies. It should be noted that these strategies cannot be learned just by reading about them. To learn how to use these strategies effectively, you need to practice them.

- Fundamental analysis- Investors describe fundamental analysis as the lifeblood of investment. As you can see, this is considered a very important strategy. Fundamental analysis deals with the basics or the fundamentals. The key to using this strategy is acquiring quality information. As the saying goes, "Knowledge is power." The more quality information that you have, the more likely that you can come up with the right trading decisions. When you use this strategy, you have to analyze the different factors that can affect the prices of currencies, such as the economy, market competition, latest trend, technological advancements, and market behavior, among others. Therefore, when you use this approach, you should be updated with the latest news.

Here is an example of how you can apply fundamental analysis: Let us say that the employment rate in the United States has just increased. All other things being equal, then it is most likely that the price of the US dollar will also increase. Once you have this information, then you can take appropriate actions to take advantage of the situation.

It is also suggested that you check the record of currency inflows and outflows, which is usually published by the central bank. Fundamental analysis is probably the strategy that demands the most time and effort; however, it is also a highly effective strategy. In fact, it is so important that if you are really serious about making money with forex trading, then experts say that you should definitely learn and apply this strategy regularly. It should also be noted that this strategy can be combined with another strategy or strategies. Last but not least, keep in mind that you should focus on the quality of information over the quantity.

- Technical analysis- If you think that you are a visual type of person, then you might enjoy using technical analysis. The strategy involves analyzing graphs and charts. These visual tools show the price movements of a currency. The idea behind this strategy is that the different factors that affect a currency have their final effect on the price. For this reason, by analyzing even just the price movements, you also get to deal with all the factors affecting a specific currency. Technical analysis is like the simplified and visual version of fundamental analysis.

When you use this strategy, it is important that you learn how to identify and take advantage of patterns. But, do patterns really exist? The answer to this question is yes. In fact, even a completely random generator also creates patterns every now and then. However, you need to remember that patterns often come and go. This means that when you look at a graph or table, it does not always mean that there is a pattern to be seen. A common mistake is forcing yourself to see a pattern even when none exists. Remember that when you analyze a graph or table, you should always exercise a clear and unbiased mind.

Since forex brokers normally provide their traders with graphs and charts, this has become a usual strategy used by traders. However, even though this may seem simple, it also takes practice to learn how to use technical analysis effectively. Just like fundamental analysis, this strategy can also be combined with another strategy or strategies. In fact, many successful forex traders combine fundamental and technical analysis.

- Scalping- The aim of this strategy is to make small yet consistent profits while minimizing your risk. So, how does scalping work? As a scalper, you need to open a position and be disciplined enough to close it once you experience even a small profit. It is important that you do your research so you can identify a profitable currency to trade. Many scalpers rely on the mere volatility of the market. They know that the price of a currency pair rises and falls, so they just take advantage of it. However, merely relying on volatility alone is not enough. You need to pick the right currency pair to invest in. The best way to achieve this is by doing research.

Once you earn a small profit, you should close your position right away. A common mistake is to get greedy and continue to hold on to your position. The problem with this approach is that the volatility might work against you. Do not underestimate the volatility of the market. It is not uncommon for the price of a currency pair to experience a series of decreases. You have to be content with small gains. Even before you start using this strategy, make it clear in your mind that your objective is to earn a small profit. Do not worry; you can make other trades. Just be sure not to hold on to a position for too long. As long as you keep a position open, there is a risk that you can lose your money, so close it as soon as you realize a profit.

Since you will only earn a small profit, you will have to trade using a big amount to appreciate the small gains. So, if your account is not well funded, then this strategy might not be for you.

When you use scalping, be sure to keep a close eye on the market. If the price drops and it appears to be continuous, you might want to close out your position and just accept whatever losses you may experience. After all, there will always be risks involved regardless of how careful you may be.

- Momentum trading- This strategy takes advantage of strong price movements. When there is a strong price movement, the tendency is that it will continue for some more time. This is just enough opportunity for you to take advantage of it and make a nice profit. This approach is just like scalping in the sense that you should only aim to make a small profit. Momentum trading uses the same graphs used in technical analysis where you can observe the price movements of a currency pair. When there is a strong fluctuation in price, you cannot expect for it to correct itself quickly. The momentum of the price movement can be expected to continue for some time, and this is how you can take advantage of the situation and make a profit. If you want to use this strategy, be sure to do your research and keep a close eye on the market. Since you will be relying on the mere momentum of a price movement, you will have to act quickly. Do not underestimate the volatility of the FX market. Do not forget that this strategy relies on the momentum. Since it is just temporary trend, do not expect for it to last long. Take advantage of your position and exit the market immediately.

- Swing trading- Swing trading is a long-term strategy. This is where you hold on to a trade for a longer period. A key advantage of using this strategy is that it allows you to earn a really nice profit since you can keep a position for a much longer period. You also do not have to worry about the usual day-to-day fluctuations in the market. Of course, merely holding on to a currency pair for a long period does not guarantee you any profit. It is still important that you pick a profitable currency pair to invest in. Now, how you pick such pair is a matter of personal preference. You may want to use fundamental analysis, technical analysis, and/or others. Do what you think works for you. The important thing is to pick and invest in a profitable currency pair. It should be noted that since you will be holding on to your position for a much longer period, you need to follow the market in order to ensure the safety of your investment. If the market behavior changes unfavorably, then you might want to close your position. Just because you are making a long-term investment does not mean that you can be slack with your research. You have to be on top of your investment by following related news and the latest updates. Although swing trading is often known for allowing you to earn a high profit, this is not always the case. A high profit is possible, but it has no guarantee. In the end, it will depend on the currency pair in which you put your money. Still, earning a high amount of profit is possible. It will mostly depend on the price movement of the currency pair in the market.

- Hedging- Hedging is a protective measure against a big loss. It acts like an insurance policy in case something unexpected happens that can adversely affect your position. Although not all brokers may allow hedging, you can still find those who will allow you to hedge directly by purchasing a currency pair and at the same time placing a trade to sell the said pair. Although you may not have a net profit while both trades are open, you can still earn without having to take on additional risk simply by observing proper timing. The way a hedge protects your trade is that it allows you to open an opposite trade while you also trade the same currency pair. As a trader, you can always close your initial trade and then move on to a new trade. An advantage of hedging is that you can save your trade and even make money if the market suddenly moves against your initial position. Needless to say, if the market reverses and takes a direction that is favorable to your first trade/position, then you can place a stop on the hedging trade or simply close it, so you can easily enjoy your profits.

It is noteworthy that hedging is not advisable if you are just starting out as it is much harder to execute effectively than many other strategies. However, it is, indeed, a strategy that is definitely worth learning.

- Scaling in- The idea behind this approach is to enter a position gradually to lower your risk exposure. When you use this strategy, you will want to divide your position. For example, instead of investing a whole $100 into a single trade, you should invest in small amounts, say, start with $20. If it turns out well, then you can add another $20 or $25, and so on. This way you do not get to risk too much but still earn a profit. The drawback is that you will earn less than if you had invested the whole amount right away. By scaling in, you still earn a profit or at least minimize your losses even if the price movement suddenly becomes unfavorable. For example, if you have already profited from your first investment but the price falls after you add more funds, you will most likely end up still in a profit or at least just with a small loss. As you already know by now, it is not advisable to be too aggressive. Using this strategy is a good way to enter the market without taking on too much risk. Just like with other strategies, it is still important that you do all the necessary research to pick a profitable currency pair to invest in.

Sometimes no matter how much you study the market, it can be hard to confirm the profitability of a position although you think that it is a good trade. This is an excellent moment for you to apply this strategy, instead of missing out on a profitable position. Just be sure to do all the necessary research to ensure that the position is really worth taking.

- Scaling out- As the name implies, it is the opposite of scaling in. if scaling in is about investing more, scaling out is closing your position gradually. This is a good strategy to use if you are confident about a particular trade or investment. So, you make a big investment right away. However, if you notice that the trade is becoming unpredictable or unfavorable, you can start to lower the amount of your investment in a trade. This is an excellent way to minimize your risk. At the same time, it allows you to keep your profits and still take advantage of the price movement with a lower risk. You can start to scale out if you start to feel less confident about a position that you have or if you simply want to be more careful after making a big investment. The volatility of the market cannot be underestimated, and many things can happen in a day. So, if you ever feel like you have to reconsider your position after you have already made an investment, then you might want to scale out.

So, how would you know if you should scale in or out? Well, it depends on how the market moves, if before making an investment you are not sure if it is a good position, then you will want to scale in gradually. If it turns out to be a highly profitable position, then you can continue to scale in. Now, if you are very confident of a position, then you can invest a big amount right away. If the position becomes doubtful or if you do not feel confident about it anymore, then you can start to scale out. By learning to scale in and/or out, you get to significantly control your exposure to risk.

- Pin bar strategy- This is a strategy that you can apply when you use technical analysis. The proper time to use this is when the price of a currency pair has become stagnant over some time. When you look at a graph, this is represented by a horizontal line. Take note that the line does not have to be completely straight: Minor fluctuations in price would be acceptable. This horizontal shows that the price has become stagnant is called a *bullish pin bar.* It will stand as a support for an impending increase in price. It should be noted that it means that there is *most probably* an increase that is going to take place; however, there is no assurance that there will indeed be any price increase. In order to increase your chances of success, you should not just rely on the graph alone. This is the best time for you to combine this strategy with fundamental analysis so that you can have a better understanding of the market.

- Averaging down- If you want to make an investment at a "bargain," price then you should learn about this strategy. This is also an excellent strategy to use if you want to earn a high profit. When you use this approach, you need to pick a currency pair whose price will most likely increase in the near future. You should then invest in this currency pair. If the price increases immediately, then you can cash out and enjoy your profit. But, if the price drops, then according to this strategy, you will have to put money into it. If the price falls again, then continue to invest even more, so on and so forth. Okay, this may seem like you are making a bad investment, but you are actually making a profitable investment. How? Just imagine how much you will earn if the price of the said currency pair is able to recover either back to its original price (the rate when you first applied this strategy) or higher. As you can see, when this happens, all the buy orders or additional investments that you have made will realize a nice profit. As you can see, this is a highly practical and profitable strategy. However, it should be noted that it is also considered an aggressive strategy, so you need to be cautious when you use this approach. There is a chance that the rate of a currency pair might not be able to recover. If this happens, you will most probably encounter a bad loss. This is why it is important that you do all the necessary research before you even start to make any trade or investment. Due to the highly aggressive nature of this strategy, it is advised that you use this strategy sparingly. Be sure to be up to date with the latest developments in the market, especially with the currency pair that you have invested in. Take note that this strategy is not just about observing a currency pair, but you also need to study the market so that you can take more appropriate actions.

- If you want a strategy that is practical and can give you a nice profit return, then you will want to master this one. Just do not forget that averaging down is also an aggressive strategy, so use it carefully. Just like with the other strategies, picking the currency pair to invest in is a crucial part of this strategy. After all, there is no way to make a profit unless you pick the right currency pair. Take as much time as you need when you do your research. Once you start to use this strategy, you should be ready to invest a significant amount of your funds.

- Forex wedge breakout- There are many breakout strategies that you can find. With this one, you need to find a wedge pattern where the price increases and decreases. However, unlike the usual wedge, you will see that the differences between the price increase and decrease diminish over time. This means that if the pattern continues, then it will be a mere horizontal line. The idea is to take advantage of this pattern before it turns into a horizontal line. Hence, you should open a position immediately after a price decrease. Take note that you should not be greedy and hold on to a position for a long time; otherwise, you will lose profit due to the volatility of the market. Be conservative and be satisfied with a small gain. Be ready to close your position once you profit by a few pips. You will most likely see a lower profit than the previous increase since the trend gradually turns into a horizontal line, but it is still a profit nonetheless.

- Conservative- This approach encourages you to be conservative when you engage in the forex market. Do not make trades that are aggressive, especially those trades that are not backed up with sufficient research. When you use this strategy, you should focus on making small but multiple successful trades. Do not focus on how much you will earn per trade. Instead, focus on how you can increase your rate of success. It is advised that you use the same amount per investment trade. Start out small. Once you have more confidence in your strategy, then you can easily increase the amount of your investment per trade. It is important that you take a conservative approach. Although there are no hard and fast rules as to what is considered conservative, many experts agree that you should keep your trade to not more than 5% of your total funds per trade. Starting out small and being conservative is also a good way to prevent your emotions from clouding your judgment. This is also a good strategy if you want to stay longer in the market. Be satisfied with small profits and aim for consistency. Once you gain more confidence, you can easily increase the amount that you invest per trade but keep in mind not to exceed the 5% ceiling per trade.

- Go with the flow- Many times, the best way to deal with the forex market is simply to go with the flow. For example, if the US market is booming, then it is a good time to invest in US dollars, especially if the economy of the paired currency does not show signs of development. When you use this strategy, it is important that you follow on the latest news as the news usually reveals important details about the market. Needless to say, you have to analyze the information that you gather. Although going with the flow can be profitable, it should be noted that you must not completely rely on what other people say about the market. To increase your chances of making a profit, you should also make your own study and analysis of the forex market.

You are not limited to the news when you use this approach. It is also suggested that you join and participate online groups and forums on forex trading. This is a good way to learn new ideas and opinions from other traders. From time to time, you will definitely find something interesting.

- Copy trade- There are brokers that offer a copy trade feature. This will allow you to copy the trades of other traders. You will be the one who will pick the trader whose trades you want to copy. When you use this strategy, you have to choose an experienced and successful trader among the majority of traders who either earn a little or even lose their investment.

A good way to do this is by checking the profile page of a trader. Once you are on his profile page, look at his success rate. If possible, view his current open positions and make your own analysis to gauge if the trader really knows what he is doing. Again, having your understanding of the forex market is still important. Once you are able to identify a really skillful and successful trader, then all it takes is a few clicks of a mouse to follow and copy all his trades.

Another way to use copy trading is by plotting the trades as well as the success rate of a certain trader. It should be noted that you will not find a trader with 100% success rate, except of course if he is just a new trader who has not yet encountered any losing trades. So, the key is to track his trades and only join him if you think that his trade is going to be successful. By doing this, you can "skip" the trades that will most probably not turn out favorably. Be careful since it is not always easy to speculate when a trader will lose or win a trade. This is a good time to make your own analysis and look for certain behavioral trading patterns. Still, it is worth noting that even though there are people who are content with copying the trades of other people, it is strongly advised that if you are serious about being a successful and professional forex trader, then you should only use this strategy sparingly. You must learn to depend on your own understanding of the market.

- Make your own- Even though there are many forex strategies that you can find, experts agree that you should learn to develop your own strategy. Take note that the best approach depends on the circumstances in the market. Hence, you have to use a strategy that is flexible and effective at the same time. You can simply modify and develop existing strategies that you already know but you are also free to come up with a strategy that is completely of your own. The strategy that you use is not as important as how much you earn from it. In the end, it is the amount of profits that you earn that matters, if any. It also does not have to be complicated to be effective. After all, trading currencies is not supposed to be a complicated activity. If you come to think about it, it is mostly just about identifying the right currency to invest in. You have to speculate whether the value of a particular currency will increase or decrease against the other currency in a pair.

Do not expect to come up with your own strategy quickly. It usually takes time to develop an effective strategy. To test how effective a strategy is, you should test it in a live market. This is a good time to use the demo account provided by your forex broker. It is also not uncommon for strategies to change just as the market also changes. Hence, if you are serious about becoming a professional forex trader, then you should be ready to continuously work on your strategy.

Chapter 5:
Best Practices

- Research- It is true that most traders do their research before they enter a trade. However, a common mistake is failing to do sufficient research. Just because you have researched the market for an hour does not mean that you are prepared to make a sound trading decision. Many professional traders spend hours every day analyzing the market, and yet they are still very careful when they enter any kind of trade. They know that a single mistake can make a big difference. Professional traders do not rely on luck. They know the importance of having quality information. This is why doing fundamental analysis is very important. If you want to be successful as a trader, then doing fundamental analysis should be a part of your day-to-day life as a forex trader.

As a rule, you should not enter any trade if you are not completely confident of your position. Remind yourself that you have no obligation to always enter into any trade. However, when you do, be sure that you are on top of it. This is the big difference between beginners and well-experienced traders. Beginners make a trade and hope to make a profit, while successful traders do so with at least 90% certainty that they will make a profit out of it. Again, the way to do this is by doing research.

There is no hard and fast rule as to what constitutes sufficient research. However, you will know if you have made enough research if you are honestly confident of your position and if you can justify it with good reasons.

- Continuous practice- To be successful in trading currencies, you cannot just rely on reading books. It is like learning a new skill. Hence, it requires continuous practice. If you are a beginner, it is advised that you should not focus on earning money immediately. Instead, you must first familiarize yourself with the actual trading environment. Again, this is an excellent opportunity for you to use the demo account provided by your FX broker. To avoid being aggressive, beginners are also advised to start small even if they have lots of funds in their account. When you deal with the forex market, you need to be extra careful. Continue to develop your strategy. Keep in mind that the FX market is a continuously evolving and moving market. As such, you also need to work on your strategy continuously.

It can be considered that your whole life as an FX trader is a long practice. Self-development simply has no end. What is important is that you take positive actions to improve yourself. Also, before you even apply any strategy, you should first practice it until you achieve mastery. Again, merely knowing a strategy is not enough. You must also practice how to apply it properly and effectively. Even if you think that you have learned a particular strategy, you should still try to develop it further. Realize that there is no end to improving your craft.

To continue learning, then you have to continue practicing. Reading books alone is not enough. When it comes to trading currencies, actual experience is necessary.

- Do not chase after your losses- This is advice that is usually given to casino gamblers. However, it also applies when you trade currencies. A quite surprising fact is that those who are well aware of this rule still violate it. How does this happen? The thing is that it can be very tempting to chase after one's losses. This usually happens after you experience a bad loss. The tendency is to want to recover what you have lost and, since you have already spent time and effort, you also want the profit. Since you can only earn a percentage of what you invest in a trade, the tendency is to suddenly take an aggressive approach. The problem here is that becoming too aggressive is also a quick way to lose all your money. Moreover, your funds will most probably not be able to handle such aggressive approach. It is tempting to chase after your losses because there is still a chance that you might be able to recover and even make a profit out of it. However, keep in mind that the risk is also high. If you do this for a long period, then you will most likely end up losing all your funds due to its highly aggressive nature. Instead of chasing more profits, expert traders suggest that you should focus on chasing after more profits. Continue to develop your strategy and become a better forex trader. Chasing after your losses leaves you no room for error since you will be spending a big part of your funds per trade. Some people would even risk their whole funds on a single trade. Again, this is highly aggressive and risky knowing that there is no amount of preparation that can give a 100% guarantee to the success of any position.

- Writing a trading journal or diary- Although this is not considered a requirement, it still helps to write your own trading journal or diary. It will allow you to view yourself from a new perspective, from a standpoint that is free from any bias and prejudice. It is also a good way to see your strengths and weaknesses more easily. Do not worry; you do not need to be a professional writer to keep a trading journal. There are only two things that you need to remember: You should be completely honest with everything that you write in your journal, and you should update your trading journal regularly.

You are free to write everything that you want that is related to forex trading. Ideally, a journal should include your reasons and objectives. You should also write about any new knowledge or realization that you encounter along the way. In the first few weeks, you might not appreciate the importance of having a journal but be persistent! After some time, you will start to appreciate it, especially when you recognize your progress or development as a trader. Your trading journal should act as a mirror of yourself as a trader, so be sure to be honest with everything that you record in your journal. If you are not fond of writing, then feel free to use a file on your computer or even your mobile phone. The important thing is to have something that you can write in and update easily. Of course, be sure that it will be safe and secure, so that you will not lose your journal. Although not all traders use a journal, it is undeniable that there are certain benefits that you can get by writing your own trading journal. To know if this is for you, then the best thing to do is to give it a try.

- Do not be an emotional trader- Although it is good to have passion for what you do, you must never allow your emotions to cloud your judgment. Do not forget that the forex market does not have any feelings. It does not care about how you feel. In fact, it does not even know you. Remain objective at all times. If you feel like your emotions are getting in the way, then stop and do not make any trade.

Before you commence a trade or enter any position, ask yourself if you have good reasons for taking that position. Be objective and make sure that every decision you make is backed up by solid research. There are no emotions in the forex market; everything is about numbers and hard facts, so be sure to always be in control of your emotions.

To avoid trading with your emotions, you should only trade with the money that you can afford to lose. This means that you should not use the money that you need to pay for your household bills and other obligations. This way, you will not be so attached to your trades but can think objectively. If, at any moment, you notice that your mind is being clouded by emotions, stop and give yourself some time until your thoughts settle down. Remember this basic rule: Only trade currencies when you can think clearly. Do not forget that the FX market is a challenging place.

- Cash out- It is not unusual to find traders who do not withdraw their profits. The reason why they do this is to grow the funds that they have in their account. After all, the bigger your funds are, the higher will also be the potential profit. Now, although this may seem practical and reasonable, you have to understand that it is still important to cash out your profits every now and then. You should understand that the only way that you can fully realize your profits is when you turn them into cash. Otherwise, it is as if you are merely using a demo account. Also, by withdrawing your profits, you can effectively minimize your risks.

  Do not worry; you do not have to cash out all of your profits in one withdrawal. If you want, you can just withdraw 25% of your profits, leaving the other 75% to increase the funds that you use for trading. However, it is still beneficial to make a withdrawal every now and then.

- Professional approach- Many people start out trading as a hobby. Although there is nothing wrong with this, it is not the most recommended approach. Taking something as a mere hobby signifies lack of commitment and devotion. If you cannot give it enough time and effort, experts suggest that you should just be a part-time trader. The important thing is to always be professional in your approach.

- Take a break- The activities of a forex broker can be lots of fun, but it can also be very tiring in the long run. It is important that you give yourself time to rest. By giving your body enough time to relax and clear your mind, you will be a more effective trader. Now, when you take a break, do it completely. The best way to take a break is not to even think about forex trading at all or anything related to it. This is the best time for you to go on a vacation or at least enjoy a movie night with your family and friends. The more that you relax yourself the better. A short but complete break will allow you to focus more completely.

Do not use this as an excuse for being lazy. Before you take a break, be sure that you first put in some serious work. Taking a break is important, but do not abuse it. Only take a break if you deserve it.

Conclusion

Thanks for all the way through to the end of this book. We hope it was informative and able to provide you with all of the tools you need to achieve your goals whatever they may be.

The next step is to apply everything that you have learned and start turning the forex market into a goldmine of profit. Indeed, those who truly understand how the forex market works earn a decent income by trading currencies. In fact, there are those who have left their day job and trade full time. Although learning to trade currencies effectively is not very easy, every effort that you put into it is will be worth it.

It is not too late to make money in the forex market. This book as given you the keys that you need. It is up to you to put that new-found knowledge into actual practice.

Finally, if you found this book useful in any way, a review on Amazon is always appreciated!